Wasted Love

Jordan Kimberly Lueder

 leaf
publishing
house

Dedicated to Roxy:
With you, my love is never wasted.

introduction

I don't remember the last time I fell asleep without thinking about love. Unless I passed out after a night of heavy drinking, my bed has been reserved for crying over lost lovers, embracing the touch of new ones, idealizing the ones I could never have, or waiting for the ones I could.

Even as a young girl, I fantasized the feeling until it appeared in my reality as a boy with freckles trickling down his nose who spoke words as clever as the ones I read in novels. I soon realized that these fantasies failed to warn me of how dangerous falling in love could actually be.

Rather than the fairytales I watched as a child, love for me turned out to be more like the first time I got wasted on a bottle of rum.

My head was spinning as I stripped down into nothing but underwear and ran through a field of sprinklers—only to be pulled down into the dirt by this same boy I fell in love with. He had me pinned to the ground with a wide smile across his face, and despite the sting of scrapes I felt on my knees, I smiled back at him.

That was the moment I became addicted to love. I started taking shots of it until I woke up with a head full of regrets. I chain smoked it until my lungs turned black. It didn't matter how much pain I felt in the morning, I would always run back to the high that broke me the night before.

When one love ended, I felt the aching need to find another. I went from person to person and got my heart broken, blaming others for my chaos. It was during the times I had no one to love that I discovered the only one breaking my heart was me.

My journey of recovering from an addiction to love is far from over, but this book is the beginning. It helped me define real love, not only for myself but for others. Writing these poems became a source to how I could heal.

I just hope that by reading them, they could do the same for you.

trigger warning:
Poems beginning with an asterisk (*) have content involving rape, nonconsensual relations, or physical and emotional abuse.

gateway

my first love

It doesn't matter
What I say or do,
When speaking of love
I'm always reminded of you.

girls

With lips much fuller than mine,
I sat quietly at my desk as she asked me the time.

I kept my own mouth closed, such a pity
I learned to hate girls that were just so pretty.

Yet, she asked me again with a smile like candy—
Unaware of my addiction, an alcoholic to brandy.

I promise she tasted just as sweet.
Nights of us kissing was my favorite treat.

And always by morning, all was forgotten—
Afraid that the flavors would cause us to be rotten.

But, I will never forget those sugar-coated lips.
When girls ask me for the time, my heart always skips.

at first sight

I fell for him instantly.

It was as if my heart knew
He was the one supposed to break it.

to be a sky in his eyes

We would lay out on grass at night
As I counted every bright star
That I could find

My eyes remained
Glued to the sky

I told him there was more to see
Our eyes will never grasp
Such a vast thing

That's when he grabbed me by the cheek
So only he could be in my view

He whispered
I was just thinking
The same about you

my first drug

I was asked what it was like to love you
And I answered—

It was like being addicted to a drug
That craved you

Just as much
In return.

young love

To be young and in love
Does not mean to be innocent
We proved this with bottles of rum
And hours of publicized sloppy kisses

The first time would feel so long
But only lasted a few minutes
And if condoms were gone
We'd go out to steal them

Oh, but wasn't it fun
How far deep we were in it
Because now that we are grown
We can never get back that feeling

a classic fairytale

I fell in love with a wolf and was taught to please.
So, I got down eagerly on both knees.

That's when he grabbed me with his teeth—
Tearing me apart, piece by piece.

And as I took the pain, I began to see
The more he dug in, the more I didn't feel a thing.

the beginning of the end

He told me that he loved me
And I believed him.

mind or heart

I have been asked the question
As to whether I would choose to live
With only intelligence or feelings.

And there is always a strong part of me
That would give up everything, even poetry
So that I wouldn't lose my mind again.

But as long as you are living,
I will choose my heart
Every time.

when it rains

I couldn't tell
If there were tears
Strolling down my face.

So, maybe that's why
When he yelled at me to leave
And pushed me away—

I still remained there,
Getting drenched
In the rain.

strength in weakness

When you know
They are no good for you
And love them anyways—
That takes strength.

But then,
Why do I feel so weak?

to love and learn

Parents are supposed to teach you what love is,
But maybe none of us really know.

We are all taught different things,
Through sources untold.

I know that my mother was fathered
By many different men.

I know that my father suffered
Through his own mother's death.

So, I do not blame my parents
For not loving each other the way I want to be loved.

I do not blame them for trying to love,
Even though they have witnessed its flaws.

Because I'm still trying too—
Despite witnessing all the consequences through you.

once a cheater

It was only the beginning
And we were young.

You disappeared
When I was falling in love.

She spoke of you
As if you moved on.

He was there
And you were gone.

I could write more excuses,
But what's done is done.

this couldn't be love

The same air we shared
While whispering words of love—
I inhaled sharply.

His fist
Buried into me,
As I yelped out that I was sorry.

He looked me
Dead in the eyes,
As my own were watering.

And I thought this couldn't be love.
But then, he wrapped his arms
So gently around me.

romanticized

When I closed my eyes,
I saw a white picket fence.

I saw a dog.
I saw a family.
I saw happiness.

But then,
I opened my eyes
And I saw you.

not yours

My body
Your token
My thighs
You open
My lips
You steal
My breasts
You feel
My mind
You play
My heart
You betray
Try me on
I am your thing
Your dirty laundry
Not a diamond ring
Then I let you know
What's deep inside
Feelings, nausea
I can't hide
You can
You do
I guess
It's true
What was
Once all yours
Now scares you

where did you go

I see all the signs
Pointing away from you,

But my feet can't move.

I'm paralyzed at the thought
Of not being with you.

Even the wind pushes me forward—
Still, I stand my ground.

Do you see how much I fight for us?
I don't think that you do.

Because then maybe, just maybe,
You'd be standing here too.

the one that got away

I saw him cry for the first time
When I decided to walk away.

But, where was this longing
When I was willing to stay?

*your best friend

He touched me
Without my consent.

He took something from me
In my faded consciousness.

So now, he will always be
My biggest mistake—

One I didn't even get
The choice to make.

how do you throw away memories?

I tore up the movie ticket
From our first date—

The one you wrote I love you on
And scribbled your name.

It's funny how a small piece of paper
Can bring up so much pain

And no matter how much I throw away,
The memories always stay.

bi-sexuality and its complexity

I opened up with so much ease
And she was the first to make me believe
Falling in love with a girl wasn't so out of reach.

But, when I finally put my hands out
All I could see were hers tangled around
The same type of boy I warned her about.

out of love

I could not tell you what it is like to fall out of love—
I have tried so many times and failed.

The most I can tell you is this—
If you have ever fallen so quickly out of love,

Maybe you were never in love, to begin with.

timing

Poetry is my time—
Taking me back to past mistakes,
Keeping me still in present feelings of pain,
Pushing me forward to future hopes I hold onto,
And I always wonder how it is, they all consist of you.

she thought

I am stronger now
She repeated to the mirror
Until she actually believed it

But then
He came up from behind
And she turned away from her reflection

Only to find out
She was still
So weak

dying for you

There is something beautiful
About dying flowers.

Even though they are parched,
They still hold color.

Even though the wind is rough,
They still try standing.

And I'm starting to realize that maybe,
This is how I appear when loving you.

here, but not

What I don't understand
Is how you can come back into my life
And suddenly make me feel

So alone.

always and forever

We once told each other forever—
But now, all I can see is the end.

just like you

He smells like you—
Weed and cologne.

He tastes like you—
Lies on his tongue.

He touches like you—
Rough and all night long.

So, I know that just like you—
He will soon be gone.

nothing like you

His arm reaches around my body
And I want so desperately

To see that same scar
On your finger.

But, this hand
Is unfamiliar.

I notice that it is entirely free
Of any scars and the responsibility

For the ones
Left on me.

05-27-09

I thought words would be the only symbols to possess me
But you changed that the day you asked me to be yours
And when you had me counting down the days
Until you would become mine again
So when I look at the date to see
The numbers that remind me
Of everything
We were
And everything
We could have been
I get this overwhelming feeling
That I will never stop giving them meaning
And despite the time lapsed since the beginning
I will always see that sequence of numbers as the day
That completely changed the way I could love another being

yours truly

You are no longer mine.
But somehow, I remain—
Endlessly and entirely yours.

addiction

alcoholic

Love is like liquor

      I drink it with no chaser

Now I've never felt sicker

      My body heaves out my dinner

At least I'll be thinner

      He likes the body of a stripper

And I do what it takes to make him quiver

      So, I pull down his zipper

Because I'm not a quitter

      And with all things considered

I've got a pretty strong liver

a blessing and a curse

Men always think
They can teach me love,
Acting as if their presence
Is a blessing from above.

Little do they know,
That my absence is a curse
And when it comes to love
I simply never learn.

ex-wife material

I'm not a good lover.
I'm a good fucker.

I can make you hungry,
But won't make you dinner.

My body is yours—
It is my mind that wanders

And my lips make promises,
Only to distract you when I break one.

So, what makes a good wife for you?
A brunette? A mother? A yoga instructor?

I won't meet those standards—
A proper woman with good manners.

So, if you commit to me
Your heart won't throb.

But, I can always vow
Another part of you will.

pandora

Like Pandora
I do not fit into your box
I am the one to open it
Letting all the chaos escape

And that's when you learned
Trying to change me
Into what you wanted
Was a big mistake

cold hands

He asked me why I was so cold.

So, I told him that I had to be
To protect the warmth inside of me.

objectified

He buys me a single shot
And grabs at my body
As if it's in stock.

But, I need to be more drunk
To feign an interest
When I'm not.

And to him
I'm just an object,
So I simply play the part—

Heartless and lost
To the next greedy man
Willing to pay a higher cost.

sleeveless

I do not wear my heart on a sleeve
It is tucked away under my belt
Fastened twice around
Given only to those
With the key

Put me on my knees
Drive me to scream
Call out my name
Make me tame

I feel no shame
For the way that I love
Those who wear hearts like a glove
Let it slide off like sweat in hot weather

I simply know better

role play

Fingers tie around my neck.
Body clasps around mine.

Don't like being held down.
But daddy, you do it just right.

Forget common sense.
Forget ladylike.

Forget what I said.
Forget being equals tonight.

I get on my knees.
You get on your throne.

I beg for a taste.
You call me sweet, baby girl.

Promise me pleasure.
I give you control.

Only here for the moment.
Make the best of this role.

shame on me

My experience in bed
Will always be both

The reason he stays
And the reason he won't.

dating a coke dealer

I am a line of cocaine
And he inhales every part of me.

For hours, for nights, for days
He becomes a straight fiend.

Then, he has to go clean—
Out of sight, out of mind.

He only handles the intensity
For brief moments of time.

But, I know that when I'm gone
He dreams of taking a hit.

And despite how hard he tries
He will always give in.

eating a woman

Searching

For new territory

I have yet to conquer

My taste buds need replenishing

And she is holding all the water

To have her lips on top of mine

The only thought my mind offers

I guess I'll never be satisfied

Until my tongue can

Touch her

lie with me

Baby girl
You're full of lies
Using that man
As your disguise
I patiently wait
You'll cut those ties
I'll tie you back up
You'd be surprised
With all I can do
Between those thighs
Twisting and turning
Your body unwinds
I know what you want
Stop wasting my time

i've tried an all man diet and didn't like it

She told me that I was a man eater.

So, I laughed as I told her
I can eat a woman too.

the chase

When they declare the words *I love you*,
It feels like the come down
To an ending high.

While they whisper the words *maybe one day*,
And it feels like the peak
Of one beginning.

a list of drugs I take

I am an alcoholic—
A chain-smoking,
Pill popping,
Sex addict.

Then,
I met you—
One more drug
I can add to my list.

the one

I am not the one
You fall in love with.

I am the one
That comes to mind
Every so often

When you are with the one
You fall in love with.

a love for addicts

My favorite men are alcoholics,
Because I know it comes with
Much more addictions

And I can't wait
To become one of them.

meeting my match

When he tells me
That he can't love me

With a cigarette
Between his lips,

I still pull out a match
To light it for him.

love language

He speaks to me
And I don't comprehend.

But then, he touches me
And I digest every inch of his skin.

I fall so instantly
When under the sheets.

We speak the same language
When our bodies meet.

If only, the translation of words
Felt as sincere as his touch—

Then maybe, just maybe
This could've been love.

warning

I will break your heart
Or you will break mine.

There is just no in between
When it comes to loving me.

when the truth hurts

You tell such pretty lies,
When I thought that I was the one
Good with words this whole time.

But they come from your lips, so rehearsed.
Like maybe, there is another woman
Falling for your curse.

Is it weak to admit that it doesn't matter?
That as long as I have you,
You can have her.

the best I have

You're my favorite fuck,
Doesn't matter the timing.

I'll never say no,
As long as you keep me cumming.

Leftovers on my tongue—
Makes the others start running.

They can't handle the intensity
Of all that you taught me.

But you handle me so well,
So, I leave my body for your taking.

Say you'll always come back
And I'll always be waiting.

stronger than liquor

I drink to forget.

But somehow, no matter
How many shots I take—

I can never forget you.

the fire we create

A fire cannot see all that it has damaged,
Unless it is put out.

And maybe that is why,
I strive so hard to keep ours burning.

quitter

I wait here patiently,
Losing all of my senses.
You give it to me so sparingly,
Knowing that's exactly what I wanted.

You put me on edge.
I want to jump, but I know better.
You like me standing right here,
Balancing on my own affections.

It arouses you to watch me struggle
And I like to see you aroused.
When you finally meet me here,
It's an inclusion like no other.

Toxins flowing through me,
Without taking any substance.
Only hits of you when you let me—
An addiction undercover.

You leave when I want just a little more.
You arrive when I've just about given up.
So, you're just like any other drug—
Not one I should mess with.

But, just like a drug,
I never know when to quit.

hypocrite

I thought that maybe,
He could love me.

Because, his throat was as black
And his hands were as rough
His eyes were as dead
Words were as cruel
As my own.

But, he did not love me
For the same reasons.

one too many

I tell him that she wants me
And he says that we should share.

So, we take her to my bedroom
And I pretend that I don't care

That the boy I want all to myself
Will only take me in pairs.

you over me

Because, if I told myself
All of the pain you gave me
Was deserved—

Then maybe, I could keep you.

pick your poison

She orders a vodka cranberry
And he tells her that she's basic.

But, it goes down so smoothly
And maybe that is why she drinks it.

Because, after all the roughness
Men have been putting her through—

She just wants to drink her poison
And have it go down easy too.

addiction

When you keep on taking,
But never feel like you have enough.

nothing but cheap wine

Cheap wine tastes better
After the third glass.

So, maybe that's why
I always let him come back.

on to the next

Cigarettes stack on my ashtray,

Like the lovers
I let into my heart—

Despite all the toxins,

I pick up another
After one is put out.

my own touch

I thought you were poison.

So, I kept my hands
To myself.

That's when I felt
Skin deteriorate

Under my own touch.

because I will let you hurt me over and over again

I think deep down, I knew
The only way to end it all—
Was to hurt you.

withdrawals

bad habits

Oh, how quickly he becomes
Just another boy I write sad poems about.

skinned

He puts his fingers to my mouth
And I want so badly to bite down.

To taste his blood on my tongue—
Payback for all that he's done.

Instead, I let him trace my lips
As I slowly start to forgive.

He knows the power that he has—
Turns my sorrows into laughs.

So, I just can't help but to let him back in.
He does what it takes to get under my skin.

he broke my heart in Spanish

He said, *"Te quiero."*
And I asked him what it meant
He said, *"It means I love you, but not quite yet."*

sleep well

He whispered that I was the girl of his dreams,
But forgot he had insomnia.

While he was my dreams,
My day thoughts,
My nightmares,

I was just a body—
Keeping him company
Until he found another.

Then he wonders why
He can't sleep at night.

he came, he saw, he conquered

He left marks on my neck
And on my pillow, is his scent.

So now that my world is stained by him—
I can never leave, even though he did.

all the things i will never say out loud

I miss you. I want you. I'll do anything.
Please come back. Please stop leaving.
Text me. Call me. FaceTime me.
Don't love her. Love me.
I'm better, you'll see.
Was I really just another body?
I think about you so much, it's scary.
You make me want to change everything.
I promise to try harder to make you love me.

still falling

You were the one who told me to fall.
Then, you pulled out your arms from underneath me.

Now, I'm plummeting down into the depths
Of a love that does not exist.

can't let go

The worst pain
Is loving someone
While fully knowing
You are not meant
To be with them.

damaged

My heart takes a beating.
My soul weakens.
My eyes blur.

That's when I pull away
And start searching for a cure.

I feel bruises shrink with every heartbeat.
I hear my soul finally sigh with relief.
I see the pain that was endured.

But, as I slowly start to heal again,
I forget all of the lessons I have learned.

when he's gone

I sleep on his side of the bed.

That way,
I don't wake up

To seeing it so empty.

don't forget

Love yourself.
Respect yourself.
Leave him.
Ignore him.

It's all so easy to say.
It's all so easy to read.

But then, he looks at you.

Your mouth is dry.
Your vision a blur.

It's all so easy to forget.

does your soul speak too?

I close my eyes and you still appear,
Despite your body not being near.

This is why I believe in souls—
Somehow ours stay intermingled.

Fondling over past love,
Embracing that old touch,

Hoping for our bodies to meet again—
And I always wonder if I should listen.

if my body could talk, we would argue

My body shouts,
"Don't let him back in!"

"But, what about love?"
I always question.

And then, it gives me
The biggest of sighs—

"My dear, you wouldn't recognize love,
If it looked you straight in the eye."

just another fix

He told me I was his favorite drug.
And now that I have experienced addiction,
I don't know why I ever saw that as a compliment.

still waiting

He told me to wait for him,
As if I haven't been waiting

For someone to love me
Since my first taste of it.

give and take

He came back with less than before.
But maybe, I was becoming so much more.

Because, all he wanted was to take what I had.
And still, I gave it to him
Just like that.

*this is not consent

I tell him I can't lose hours of sleep.
Yet, he slips in with me
Under the sheets.

That's when his hands
Go up my shirt and in my pants,
On my breasts while grabbing my ass.

I scoot away.
But, the gesture isn't good enough
And now his are getting quite rough.

I say I'm not in the mood.
He keeps asking me why—
Making it harder and harder to deny.

So, I stop my sobs with a pillow,
And turn my back towards him.
How could I let this happen again?

please,

I tell him
To leave me alone
But, do I really want him to?
I don't know.

i'm drunk

When I'm drunk
Your name becomes
My favorite noun.

It just spills out
As more shots
Go down.

Maybe, when I'm sober
I will finally learn how
To shut my mouth.

But, for now
I'm too drunk
And you spill out.

it's a trap

You get mad at me
For not speaking the truth,

When you have abused me
For speaking it in the past.

cigarettes

A man once told me
"A cigarette will take five days off your life."

So now, I smoke each one
Hoping it will be five less days
Of thinking about you.

the flowers you gave me are finally dead

I heard you bought her flowers
A week after I was in your bed.

But, what happens when
Those flowers are dead?

Will you have already moved on—
Planting seeds into another woman's head?

Maybe, I was jealous at first.
But, I decided to be grateful instead.

While she is only at the beginning
Of their life and death,

I have finally reached the end.

in return

I love you,
But I'm ready
To be loved in return.

So, I must let you go.

to those that say I deserved better

Have you ever felt so much rejection—
By the same lips that spoke of your perfection?

Have you ever been punched in the gut—
By the same hands that once lifted you up?

Have you ever been so confined—
By the same eyes that promised a lifetime?

I know I deserved better.

What I need to know is this—
Why didn't he?

bloody

I could write so much about love.
My fingertips bleed the blood I have shed for love.
While men bleed for their country, their work, their pride—
I bleed for these damn men.

numb

Sometimes, I wish you knew
All the pain you put me through.

But, your eyes remain dull.
You feel nothing at all.

So, really it's you
I should feel sorry for.

maybe

A pause in a song
Not fitting the mood

A dropped or missed call
Never returned to

A scribbled rough draft
Thrown in the trash

A halfway smoked cigarette
Burning to ash

Maybe his mood will change
Maybe his phones on silent
Maybe he'll regret what he did
Maybe he'll pick up that old habit

Don't wait on the maybes
Don't waste precious time

If he wanted more of you
He wouldn't have left you behind

lovesick

I feel my heart
Dropping down
To my stomach

And I want nothing more
Than to throw it up.

I would rather see it sitting
In a pool of vomit

Than feel it beat so rapidly
Inside of me.

But, I've done that before—
Thrown out my heart
To whoever caught it.

It doesn't matter the person,
They always become the vomit.

This time
I will keep it down.

Within my organs it will remain safe.
They can't become another mess I have made.

irony

I'm trying to forget you,
But I have to remind myself every day.

the weight of it all

I would have given you everything—
My heart, body, and soul.

If only you were strong enough
To carry it all.

no more happy endings

Do not give a man in bed
What he fails to give
Outside of it—

Attention, commitment
And a happy ending.

Do not give a man
What he fails to give
In bed—

Attention, commitment
And a happy ending.

to the moon and back

Sometimes I wonder
If the moon can hear my thoughts
When I look up at it.

And if it did,
You must have a lot of explaining to do
When you look up at it too.

for him

You have given me
So much to write about

And I can't decide

If I should thank you
Or hate you for it.

for her

I was not ready for you—

Just as much as you
Were not ready for me.

don't come back

You were my hardest goodbye.

So please, do not come back
Only to make me do it
All over again.

the problem

I have no problem
Finding someone to love.

I have no problem
Finding someone to love me.

The problem is
Finding someone to love
That loves me in return.

when does it end

The love I have for you.
The tears that I shed.

The hurt in my heart.
The lies in my head.

These are the things
That don't seem to end,

Even though
We did.

maybe I never will

Falling in love with you
Was the easiest thing I could ever do.

Falling out of love with you
Is the hardest thing I have yet to get through.

homeless

She was my home.

So, when she decided to leave
I have become nothing but a beggar
As I wait for her to come back to me.

the story of a poet in love with an illiterate

You said that
If I wrote a book

It would be the only one
You would ever read.

At first, I thought
This to be sweet.

But now that we are over,
You won't read a single thing.

And I am left to wonder
How I could ever

Fall in love with a man
Who could not read.

myself

I have been liking myself a lot more lately—
The self that no longer belongs to you.

heartbreaker

I have been called a heartbreaker.
But, I wonder if people ever consider
How many times my heart has been broken
For me to become this way.

goodbyes

The moment you realize
That the past you created together

Will always be better
Than the future you could have

rehabilitation

breakthrough

And then I realized,
I was no longer crying about him.

I was crying about all that I lost
When I was with him.

mind over matter

You can love someone
And not want to be with them.

You can crave their touch
And not desire their presence.

That is the complexity of emotions
Playing every part of you.

Ultimately, it is your mind
That makes the decision.

I won't love you anymore.

just admit it

You may never admit
To hurting me.

But, every day
You will wake up

Feeling guilt in your heart,
Never knowing how to rid of it.

the bright side

I am trying to see
The bright side of our love.

But, I can't seem to find it
Within all the darkness
That we created.

skin deep

There is so much more to me
Than what can be touched and held.

My soul is longing
With good intentions.

My heart is heavy
With so much to give.

But, you only wanted my skin
And feared its blemishes.

You only wanted my body
And feared its weight.

Seeing that fear is when I knew
I didn't want any of you.

don't come back a third

The first time you left,
I felt so much pain.

The second time you left,
I felt so much relief.

less is more

When I lost you,
I found myself.

It does not make you any less.
It has simply made me more—

So much more.

12am

I don't think
I've experienced
Anything as freeing
As going an entire day
Without thinking about you.

it was never about you

He told me to stop writing about him—
To forget his name.

And I would love nothing more
Than to rid of him in everything I create.

But, my heart still bleeds onto pages
From the cuts he has made.

My hands still ache to release
The weight he has placed.

I know that he doesn't deserve
To be the muse to my pain.

But, I deserve to let it out
Until he is completely erased.

you lost

I may have loved and lost,
But at least I loved.

That's something you could never say.

playerism

He says he loves my poetry
As he tries to scoot
Closer to me.

He says my words are inspiring
And to be disappointed by men
Must be so tiring.

To be honest it is,
And he is an example of this.

See the words I have written are true,
Unlike the ones he speaks to you—

When trying to get into your head.
When trying to get into your bed.

So, he can keep trying to use
The same lines over and over again
To captivate me.

But, I will always use my own
Written within these pages
As a reminder to leave.

she has more power than he can ever give

He can make a woman so strong,
But instead makes her weak.

When she comes to realize this,
She will finally leave—

Only to become much stronger
Than he could have ever made her to be.

she deserves better

She tells me she wants more—
You are not giving enough.

But, she is latched on
Like a flower's roots to soil.

Her nectar produced
By sparse compliments.

Her stem fed
By cheap take out.

Her petals bloomed
By fleeting touch.

She does not know the power
Of finding her own ground.

Oh, but once she does
You will regret it.

Soil is nothing but dirt
Without the roots of a flower.

she is so needy

Learn to satisfy her needs,
Before she learns to need nothing
And decides to leave.

but will he even notice

When there are days
He makes you feel
Like the only girl
In the world.

And there are days
He makes you feel
Like you don't
Even exist.

Maybe,
It is time
That you don't—
Not in his life anyway.

he will notice

If he makes you feel small—
Show him how big you really are
And walk away.

seeing the light

I thought you were my light,
But as I dived in further
It only became darker.

I thought love should be deep,
As deep as the ocean,
Until I swam to the surface.

I thought I did it all wrong
When I cursed to the sun
And that's when it told me:

Love does not make you swim to the depths—
Causing you to be breathless,
But lifts you up to help you breathe again.

good luck

You don't get to keep me
Until you find someone better.

Because, I wait for no one
And you'll be looking forever.

too late

When I decided
To love myself,

You decided
To love me too.

But, loving myself
Could only happen

By leaving you.

love or let go

If it hurts to love them,
Let them go.

what if doesn't exist

You were my what if.

Now, you are nothing
But a why.

it's the hold

You keep trying
To give away your heart
And watch it slip
Through fingers.

Grasps wet
From sweat,
You make them
Too nervous.

Even dry palms
Let it fall to the floor,
Distracted by
Their own thirst.

But, don't
Give up.

There will be
A pair of hands,
No matter how
Wet or dry,

They won't let
The damned
Thing
Go.

bisexuality

A boy once told me
I could not love him
If I was attracted
To girls.

A girl once told me
I could not love her
If I have been with
So many boys.

I was a fool for trying to convince them.

Because, one day I will fall in love
And they will believe me.

pink and blue

When I see clouds of pink
Floating within a blue sky's crease,

I am reminded of my lovers—
Consisting of both hims and hers.

And if God didn't think that was right
Then why, oh why, is it written in the sky?

to die for

Find the one
You would die for.

Find the one
Who will never let you.

distractions

And what is it like,
Without all the distractions?

When you're sitting there,
Face to face—

Without drugs in your veins,
Alcohol on your breath,
Smoke in the air,

Without television,
Killing out the silence.

Because there is a difference
Between loving someone
And loving someone being there.

it's okay to miss them

There are some people
We are meant to miss,

Because they will always be
Far better in our minds

Than they could ever be
In front of our eyes.

feeling distant

If you become distant
From yourself

The closer
You get
To him

He is not
The one

the main character

There are some people you are meant to write novels about
And there are some you are meant to write chapters on.

Then, there are those who hide in between the lines
And there are those who never quite make the edit in time.

But, no matter who ends up in each of these roles
Remember that it is your story that's being told.

keep her wild

I no longer want to be chased—
Only to be caught and set free.

I want someone willing
To run wildly with me.

please understand

I need my lover to understand that I'm an introvert—
I can go days without speaking to them.

I need my lover to understand that I'm depressed—
I can go days without speaking to anyone.

I need my lover to understand that I'm a writer—
I can go days without speaking at all.

weathered

I preferred the sun,
While you complained of the heat.

Now, I look up at the clouds
And think of how happy you must be.

This must be the feeling
Of accepting a lost lover,

Because even though
I hate this weather—

I'm still so glad
That it exists.

If only for you
To enjoy it.

it's not you, it's me

To those
I could not love,
Because I did not
Love myself—
I am sorry.

And to me,
Because I thought
They could make me
Love myself—
I am so sorry.

to be a writer

If only I could say
All the words that I write.

Then maybe,
I would not be
So misunderstood.

But, because I write
More than I speak—

I understand myself
More than anyone
Ever could.

lessons

I have learned that love
Is not supposed to change me,
But make me more of who I already am.

first true love

It was when I fell in love with myself
That I finally realized—

This is my first time truly loving
And being loved in return.

the next one

To write this book,
It took a lot of heartache
And gallons of liquor.

I just hope the next one
Will take a whole lot of love
And a single glass of wine.